August Autumn

Acknowledgements

Some of these poems have appeared in: *Ambit, Boston Review, Critical Quarterly, Delta, Encounter, The Honest Ulsterman, London Magazine, Mandeville Press Dragoncards, New Poetry 3, 4* and *6* (Arts Council), *New Statesman, The Penguin Book of Light Verse, Peterloo Anthology 1, Phoenix, Poetry Durham, Poetry Now* (Radio 3), *Poetry Review, Poetry Society Newsletter, Quarto, Samphire, South West Review, Tomorrow* and *The Times Literary Supplement.*

A selection was included in *Poetry Introduction 5* (Faber and Faber).

August Autumn

Duncan Forbes

Secker & Warburg
London

First published in England 1984 by
Martin Secker & Warburg Limited
54 Poland Street, London W1V 3DF

British Library Cataloguing in Publication Data

Forbes, Duncan
August autumn.
I. Title
821'.914 PR6056.06/

ISBN 0-436-16138-9

To Debbie

Printed in Great Britain by
Paradigm Print, Gateshead
Tyne and Wear

Contents

Acknowledgements

If at the front of his first published book
Acknowledgements are brief as mine would be,
Then for both book's and author's dates I look
And if their difference makes him old as me,
I count the poems on the contents page
And then divide the total by the years
Less the first twenty of the poet's age,
And if his annual output somewhere nears
My chronic shortage, I will read a verse,
But never a whole poem, and pronounce
That my work's excellent since his is worse,
Or his is so good that mine hardly counts.
But even such assessment's a precaution
In case success and merit bear proportion.

Deposition

Christ's body smelt of Goddard's Silver Dip
When as head prefect not as sacristan
I carried at school Eucharists the cross
Up to the gilt one on the reredos
Where as a new boy near the servers' stalls
I had admired, compelled to be at worship,
Those mutually exclusive optionals
Of Art and Carpentry in unison.

But outside chapel crucifixions hurt.
They tied you by the wrists to clothing hooks
Which kept your head still so you could be gagged
With a taste of hand, until you'd been debagged.
Compared to this, I saw Christ crucified
In terms that sermon cricket could convert
To signalling a universal Wide,
Which I still bowl and on which he still looks.

For, seeing a woman on a London bus
Each of whose earlobes was a crucifer,
– Since flat gold crosses dangled from her ears
Which painlessly no doubt she'd once had pierced –
All I do now, now flesh and symbol meet,
Is wonder if, to keep them free of pus,
She sponged with cotton wool swabs from a pleat
An antiseptic on her stigmata.

The duty officer at Calvary,
Who stood the closest to the prisoner's side,
Is reckoned by two gospels to have said,
"This was the Son of God", once Christ was dead.
So later if he heard without conviction
What else there was to Christianity
I hope he never thought the Crucifixion
Was when he'd just wished well of one who died.

Xmas

At the decree of Caesar
Morecambe and Wise combine
Into a two man donkey
To fetch from Palestine
Joseph, Mary and Jesus
To British pantomime.
There are no flights to Egypt
For Jewish refugees,
Nor could they get a visa
At this troubled time
And if they stay in Bethlehem,
The guest star guarantees
That wicked uncle Herod
Will kill the under-threes.

Mary solves the problem
Of Christmas cards this year
With a notelet that announces
Her baby boy is here.
His weight in pounds and ounces,
His name, Jesus Christ,
And his birthdate, Christmas,
Are given in a list.
Even cards for charity
She finds overpriced.
And as for Christmas presents
Everything's so dear,
She's come to an arrangement
Of none at all this year.

At the decree of Caesar
All the world and his wife
Go home or have their parents
For family Christmas strife,

And hope comes out of the freezer
Though it never comes to life.
So while the icebound Santas
On halves of Christmas cakes
Watch Christmas trees die thirsty,
Every agnostic makes
A New Year's Resolution,
One that he always breaks,
Not to observe next Christmas
For Christ's or Caesar's sakes.

Sister

Though neither of us ever stood
As straight as mother wished we would,
I stood up straight for, but I lost,
The brother-sister back to backs
Which mother refereed with books
And which I always hoped you'd lose,
You six-foot-tall hypotenuse.

Height was an issue less alive
When I was six and you were five,
Yet at a fancy dress parade,
Crawling behind you on all fours
I wished my mask had proper jaws
Because my wolf was not as good
As you, you smug Red Riding Hood.

And even when we went to school
We learnt no equalising rule,
Since your best subject was my worst
And you sat in and did for fun
The Maths that I was coached to learn.
So what made you turn Classicist,
Except that I had started first?

But then you won, to my disgrace,
The year I gained an Oxford place,
Your exhibition to St Anne's.
Though I resented you there more
After I'd found you in my room
Getting much further with a man
Than I'd got girls on that divan.

When people asked if we were twins
I matched our sallow, greasy skins,
Brown hair, brown eyes and lanky stance,
But now I wonder if they meant
Some symmetry of temperament,
Caused not so much by common genes
As competition in our teens.

So now I've got, while you have none,
A younger sister for my son,
I hope that they'll be different,
But let's hope, if they do compete,
They're sooner to admit defeat
Than both their father and their aunt,
Who haven't done so, till they can't.

Helen

The rape of Helen and the sack of Troy
Began the odyssey of boarding school
With Latin bullying my mother tongue.
My sister, Helen, took a week to die,
My mother said, but I'd have been too young
To learn that in her backbone was a hole.
The bachelor Latin master who could cane
Taught the new Helen to a homesick boy.

And I imagined on the Trojan mound
A rampart crippled like a malformed spine
Round the cremated body of the town,
And when the Trojans saw the empty plain
Or Menelaus heard that she had gone,
Their legendary sorrows spoke for mine.

Alexander Wilson

My middle two names may make you laugh,
But I was christened to bury the dead,
I am the family cenotaph
For the younger brother my mother had.

He was the man in the photographs,
The smart lieutenant of the 12th Black Watch,
He was the ghost in the negatives
Whose uniform haunted the dressing-up box.

Somewhere in Burma, freckled, red-haired
And hot in new khaki, he died in my stead.
Monsoons were his mourners, his epitaph mud.
By the time he was my age, he was seven years dead.

Prep School Grounds

Each of the trees in Kennedy's gender rhymes
Plus many non-Indo-European species
Grew Latin nameplateless in the school grounds.
So the first trees we learnt there were as climbs,
Not masculine, feminine or neuter nouns.
Balsa alone came extra to the fees
From an Aylesbury shop in precut pieces,
But otherwise all other then-known trees
Had either bark or branches we could grip –
All but the sumachs which were out of bounds.
    Yews blackened sweat and inked in palmistries,
The cedars leaked a sap like balsa glue.
Redwoods we sprinted at with skewers of box,
Each trying to stab the trunk highest with his.
We used scots pine branches to sweep an airstrip
From which, between an ash and conker tree,
Holding toy planes to fir-cone bombs we flew.
But the only play in the woods there that connected
Genders and trees were games of Off-ground He
Where the headmaster's daughter, Rosalind,
Was too slow to be worthwhile making It.
    Her father taught us later in Top Form
With our long trouser turn-ups full of twigs
That though there were exceptions to the norm
French trees were male, and Latin feminine,
And here for once he thought the Romans right.
The tallest trees, climbed only by the wind,
Were what I fell for: elms at their full height
Were substantives that made me adjectival,
Without attracting me in a sexual way.
For though those elm trees, pines and poplars lent
The school its *Graf Spee* on the skyline shapes
For miles around, they supervised survival,
Since they'd endured from that long holiday
Before each bedroom had become a dorm,
Before the wallbars and the fire escapes.

Butterfly Collection

My shadow sidled next to me on tiptoe,
While one Red Admiral spread embroidered wings,
Its hair-spring tongue unspiralling to tipple
Scented liqueurs. Robed for investiture,
In doctoral red, white, black and blue, it sunbathed,
Hinging upon its whiskered fuselage
Wings deckle-edged as pencil sharpener shavings.
Slowly I wiped my hands against my shorts,
Triggered my thumbs and cupped my fingers airtight,
Then waited for the butterfly to fold.
With a sudden snarl of bees and whiff of buddleia,
A tickle clattered in the dark I held.

Indoors was cool and twilit as a larder.
The glass gas-chamber of my screw-top jar
Stank of ammonia drunk by blotting paper.
Closed on the lid, the butterfly at first
Hung passive like a flake of blackened leaf-mould.
A wingtip shivered. Repulsively
Its nose-haired abdomen inflated, writhing.
It dropped, capsized, kicked filaments of leg.
Wings flapped as if on fire, but fanned an ember
Which hovered, hopped and scuttled round the jar.

My breathing pivoted its hand-held deadness,
Till at its wings' clenched colour plates I tugged.
Dusty pigment marked my fingers guilty.
I fractured its dihedral, just to feel
The smudged transparencies that glazed its wingspan.
Then judging the specimen as not for show,
I dropped dismantled bits into a matchbox.
Yet, shut in the dark myself, I couldn't sleep,
But breathed the stuffy air beneath the blankets,
And cowering there in dread of it I prayed
That when it found me the avenging angel
Would smother first whom it would mutilate.

Requiem

With crowded mourners and surpliced priests
Sit those who were once our wedding guests,

The stern archdeacon who married us
Offers the funeral address,

And where your father read our banns
Is an empty step where his coffin stands.

The same black fleet of cars on hire
Brought him and the bridal party here

And he found it difficult not to cry
As I do, biting back tears, today

At this sad marriage of love to grief,
This funeral of a married life.

He gave you away in ritual loss:
If he were here he could comfort us.

Mother and Son

Murals of the sunset
Search the eastern wall.
On the purple carpet,
By a wad of cotton wool,
A young boy stands naked,
Spotty and irritable.

His mother goes and fetches
The bottle of calamine,
Then dabs the hot red blisters
Of chicken-pox on his skin
With pink cooling blotches
On his buttocks, legs and spine.

She patiently kneels, anointing
Each pox that is driving him wild,
Almost as if she were painting
Her own *Madonna and Child*
And the scars she was preventing
Would leave him undefiled.

Fatso & Spotty

Do you look like the woman
Loafing on the sand,
With the shot-putter's bosom,
A doughnut in her hand,
And a massive bathing costume
Which must have been custom-built
To hide her jumbo bottom
In a pink pelmet of kilt?

Or am I like the weakling
With acne on the brain
Diffidently cycling
Uphill against the rain,
Hair lank with natural greases,
Lips mouthing a teenage grudge,
Grim old-fashioned glasses,
Face a pustular smudge?

If he is not my double
And you are not obese,
Why are we both unable
To let such questions cease?
Would Fatso or Spotty
Like to hear the truth?
You have a perfect body
If I am a spotless youth.

Nude

The door is open and yes she is naked,
The blonde at the basin cleaning her teeth.
I and her toothbrush are over-excited;
I could catch her quivering rump and eat it
Now as she steps through the steam to the bath.

Her skin wears a two-piece of next to no suntan.
And striped in brown and orange (just like mine)
A flannel, saving energy for later,
Floats in the warm promiscuous water.
Soap and flannel are lucky men.

Sweat on the mirror. Soap in its slime.
Waters have issued, the plughole has moaned
And the bath is empty except for the scum,
The dead hairs, puddle and dirty rim.
She was on two counts not a real blonde.

Learning to Drive

In the revised and pricier *Highway Code*
No marriage guidance counsel was included.
So I taught you parking in a No Through Road.
I drew a diagram, but you pooh-poohed it,
Preferring with both kerbside wheels to clamber
Backfirst half onto the pavement. Thus back we crawled,
Till I yanked on the handbrake and we stalled,
Me blaming you, and you me and the camber.

On our next trip, at a disused aerodrome,
We practised aim, but you discovered speed,
And passed your first lorry on the journey home.
The licence you now hold means I can map-read
While you are driving. But I sometimes still
Find my right foot automatically braking
When you are on the point of overtaking,
As if I dually controlled your will.

Greetings

"Hello. Rare sight. Where've you been sheltering?"
Cornered like that I dodge by murmuring,
"Scarcity value" or "Well camouflaged":
        Something to show I do not need
My cushions patted, like an invalid,
Nor do I want my scabbiness massaged.

Besides, what have I done to bring on me
The throttling bandage of his bonhomie?
Am I the Yeti to be shot at sight?
        Must a press conference be held
Each time I step into the outside world?
Am I the victim of my own Apartheid?

What I object to really is the guess
Which labels me so wrongly when he says
First to himself, then me, "Here's our recluse."
        My flimsy cordiality
At that, is to him further proof. To me
It shows I'll talk where and with whom I choose.

But given the seclusion he thinks mine
I see myself picked out as next in line
To teach this Century its A B C.
        To live peered at in formalin,
A common though elusive specimen,
Is not the life for the eclectic me.

August Autumn

Ever since the news,
Your father has been obsessed
By individual trees
And the dying avenues
Which have caught Dutch elm disease.
Elms with jaundiced leaves
And stains of nicotine
Throughout the diocese
Are changing their natural green
To an August autumn brown;
And elms with no leaves at all
But rookeries scribbled among
The neat, botanically-drawn
Dead upper branches and twigs
Bring winter suddenly near.
These will have to come down
And quickly before they fall,
He says in his car beneath
With his father's walking stick
Beside the driving seat
As the only outward sign
Of the cancer in his lung
And the cancer in his spine.

At night when we go to bed,
My folded sweater prays
And my trousers genuflect
Over my bedroom chair
In attitudes of faith,
But the thoughts I try to collect
Until I drop off to sleep
Refuse to offer a prayer
To a hypothetical God.
Yet I will your father's escape

From a death of cancerous pain
And the dull uncomfortable ache
In his lower vertebrae
That wakes him or keeps him awake.
I have seen him preach to the mad
In a women's mental home,
Where he joined his hands to shape
An arrowhead on its way
To the heart of his Christian God,
And showed them how they could pray
The "Our Father" like the sane.
But what will his God become
If the cancer attacks his brain?

As he gives you the wine or bread,
After I've watched him bless
Our son's oblivious head
Up at the altar steps
Where I have never knelt,
I read the hymnbook and wait.
But I find it nevertheless
Impossible now to forget
That your father's lifelong faith
Is an indirect result
Of an earlier painful death,
And that even Christ on the cross
In his foreign dead language screamed
A God-forsaken why
When the pain became too great.
Prayerbook and painkillers lie
On the seat of the bedside chair
By your father's side of the bed:
But oh how desolate, bare,
And unbelievably dead
Will a whole hinterland seem
To my own, I suppose, despair
When he and his certitude die.

Uncertainty

Graves of husbands, wives and lovers,
Like the churchyard manhole covers,
Proudly bear their maker's name,
But they're rotting all the same
When the earth the vicar blessed
And the turves have detumesced.

Whether I or you die first –
Can't think which I've most rehearsed –
Senseless fossil pollen grains
Will date our animal remains
To the first years grass grew flowers
Over either grave of ours.

But the knowledge I shall die
Cannot also tell me why,
Nor can all there ever is,
Nor all brief posterities
From Pre-Cambrian year dot
Till the universe is not.

Sheltered Upbringing

Hydrangeas test the soil's acidity.
The mirror triptychs in the bedroom windows
Collect the light in narcissistic pools.
Safe in their Wellingtons and windcheaters
Peter and Jane are helping Daddy garden.
He clips the privet and they feed the bonfire.
Soon they will plant potatoes in its embers
And eat them, hard and gritty, after tea.
At dusk they listen to their bedtime story:
Henry The Green Engine who was immured
For disobedience like Antigone.

Day of Obligation

A growth of scaffolding on Wells Cathedral.
Saints and fossil angels have lost face.
A new Apollo at Canaveral,
Sunlight on the television mast
Points from the Mendip Moors to outer space.

The sky is endless and there is no sky.
All resurrections are deciduous
Or so the birdsong and the leaves imply.
Well, in again to cake with chocolate eggs,
Then *Murder On the Orient Express.*

National Anthem

Two undergraduates on grants
Play snap with invitation cards
During the Vietcong advance,
While some redundant patriot
Blows unemployment benefit
On one accumulator bet.

Subalterns sign, on each success,
Positions in a book on sex
Kept for the purpose in the Mess,
And weightlifters on steroids blow
Hot water bottles up for show,
Their cheeks inflating indigo.

Chiropodists as one condemn
The fashion footwear of the time,
Predict the nation's crippledom,
As a chihuahua with a squeal
Is through its inbred fontanelle
Crushed to death by a platform heel.

If it was ever in their grip,
United Nations have let slip
The planet's moral leadership.
Arcus senilis round the moon
Foretells the end of something soon
Which tidal waters will not clean.

A Naval Wife

A naval wife, driving her husband's car,
Heads for an art materials shop, to get
A blown-up photo of his carrier framed.
It shows, he wrote, the flight-deck plus a jet.
Hoped to fit more water in but I mis-aimed.

She parks by a seagull-pestered reservoir,
A type-cast backcloth for a town, half port
Half shopping-centre cum resort. The gulls
Yelling above her prompt her to recall
Dockyards at dawn, gloom, then the carrier hull's
Long shadow sliding down the jetty: all
Things which the snapshot had by proxy caught.

Two Dreams

In the first an adder,
One foot long and brown,
Basked on hill-fort pasture
Drought had done to a turn,
As I walked with my daughter
Around the dairy farm.

The other dream was odder:
I knew the woman's son;
I was his English master
And I had met her once.
Now we discussed her future
Over a buffet lunch.

The snake moved like a ripple.
I panicked for an axe
To sink into its middle –
A flash of blade and sparks
And head and tail would dribble
Writhing on dusty grass.

A Reisling stood on the table,
Lettuce and hard-boiled eggs.
The mother was suicidal:
Divorce was on the cards.
But as she peeled an apple
Had she made a pass?

My face in the shaving mirror
Is implicated still:
What Joseph said to Pharaoh
Or Jung and Freud reveal
Can never root out my horror
Of the serpent or the girl.

The Other Woman

"I thought you were the milkman.
I was going to pay next week."
"Well, may I come in? It's freezing.
I've brought back Alan's book."
I covet their central heating,
And the warmth of her physique.

Alan is out with the children,
And she tells me where. I know.
Moves as much as phrasing
Are all-important now.
She and I are sitting
Almost toe to toe.

Would I like some coffee?
If I say "Afterwards, yes,"
At worst she can beg my pardon
Or smack me on the face.
The truth is that she whispers
"All I have on is my dress."

But afterwards on the fluffy
Pelt of the fireside rug,
Should it be glowing carbon
Or lichen singed on a log
That I watch, as she brings me slippers;
Then coffee stirred in a mug?

Framed photos of my children
Smile but cannot tell,
And so to save you guessing
I may as well reveal
That I dreamt up the setting
And most of its personnel.

Alan's book, the milkman,
Weren't they a give-away?
And such salacious treason,
It had to be a lie.
Or am I in her play-acting
An equally easy lay?

At the Regal

Is there nothing better to do
On a Monday afternoon
Than watch a film about caribou
Waiting for the western to come on?
I munch sweets in the stalls and think
This is the worst film I have ever seen
As the caribou migrate across
Acres of tundra on the screen,
Cold tired and cadaverous
And as near as makes no odds extinct.

In preference to junk like that
Give me the cowboy any day –
Living where he hangs his goddam hat
And playing poker for his pay –
Yup, he could make me a brand new man
If he just complied with three small ifs:
1) if he had acne on his chin,
2) he were a part-time pacifist
And 3) he once had to ask the heroine
"Say honey, sorry, where's the can?"

That's the sort of thing I want,
Loads of authenticity:
Viz. the couple courting hard in front
Whose stifled brute activity
Excites me more than every horde
Of Hollywood Apache braves
Repelled by the US Cavalry.
Those lovers can at least paraphrase
Both my lust and jealousy,
And they aren't either hired or bored.

Wild Life Poster

Dressed like a bat for a fancy dress ball,
A SEAGULL flounders in acres of oil.
A HEDGEHOG, flattened by a radial tyre,
Bleeds through its scalp of horrified hair.
Suspected of rabies, a FOX is shot,
And it's Belsen for BADGER inside its set.
A SALMON floating with warts on its face
Lies flat on its back in industrial waste.
A SWALLOWTAIL's mad aerobatic displays
Are caused by the pep in insecticide spray.
SPRUCE is felled for journalists' froth.
SEALS are orphaned, then bludgeoned to death.
But a CROW has a live young RABBIT to eat
And starts by pecking its eyeball out.

Herd

Across the wide green water-meadow,
Their tongues and teats a fleshy pink,
The Friesians ate their stunted shadows
All the way to the river-bank.

A belly with a fraying tassel?
A young bull grazing with the herd,
Or did the kiss-curls, horn and muscle
Hide a bovine river god?

Struggle

A blackbird with a split-nib bill
Open wide at an orange angle,

But the beak deformed and the bird dumb,
Strops the lower half on an earthworm.

The mauled intestine of the lawn
Oils a salad of dandelion.

As if excited by writhing meat
The blackbird works with an appetite.

Oh the suffering of them both!
Protracted hunger and slow death.

The worm that will never feel again
Topsoil juicy after rain,

The bird that will never know at all
Berries spherical in his bill,

The answerable mating-call.

Horse

A horsebox parked by a Land Rover,
A blue saloon car with its hatchback open,
One sunlit afternoon in late October
In a paddock neither rural nor suburban.
A handsome pony with a thick blond mane
Is walked in circles past a group of men
Who might be bidding for the horse at auction.
But why the runny bloodstain on its groin?
Where is the foal if that's obstetric blood?
The small pink tube of a mollified erection
Is dangling like a teat and shakes its head,
Though why no mare if he is out to stud?
The wind strips beech trees for the coming winter.
I watch him led round, raw, domestic, neuter.

Stag

Behind iron railings,
To the rasping croup of his belling,
The harem huddles for bread,
Their black toes stuck in the mud,
Except for the doe he is following
Who will not lower her head
With that foghorn lowing and blowing
Vapours at each hindquarter
Of her already rain-licked fur.

She steps away, inches
Ahead of his antler branches,
Insisting the appetite
Grow and salivate
With the stir of her haunches.
And so they provoke and excite
Till she stops and he staunches
The open wound of her sex
With the brute force of his flesh.

Catch

A spider's web has trapped a wasp,
The denier of the net has sheared,
The angry buzz has caught a lisp,
The broderie has grown a beard.

A claw in her mosquito net,
The fierce cocoon is snarling loud.
The killer tangled in a knot
Stabs the gossamer of his shroud.

Soft Fruit

The strawberry leaves were autumn red
Nevertheless, nevertheless
In the straw of an empty bed
Where lightning whipped the frightened horse,
One late strawberry lay beneath
The fat warm teardrops of the rain,
A ruby on its hairy stem,
The eyeball of the horse insane
For shelter from the thunderstorm.

What was alive that I in fright
Took as the strawberry from the plant?
A snail was fattening on the fruit
While Miss Shapiro's tenor voice
The wet-nurse of an ammonite
Sang *Walking Back To Happiness,*
A cornucopia vivante
Indulging in a secret vice,
The client and the prostitute.

I divorce, be kind, be cruel,
Weeping berry, puckered foot
Pulled the mollusc from its meal
And by the misty Firth of Forth
Threw it in the undergrowth.
Fish and chips with tartare sauce,
Willow-herb and thistle-legs.
A train of inter-city thought
Crossed the cantilever bridge

Nevertheless, nevertheless,
Remembering the gutted snail
The berry parted from the mouth
Flesh retiring to the skull
And summer over in the North
Like Helen's teenage happiness
Which cost the fear inside the horse,
I could not bring myself to eat
The nibbled crimson of the fruit.

Neither a Tourist nor a Purist Be

In a Stratford trattoria strategically placed,
My stomach grumbled like a hungry old fogey's
For a catchpenny pizza made by Pirelli
With mushrooms and olive formed from black plastic,
Anchovies hairy as a Cypriot's bogeys,
The cooked cheese chewy as knicker elastic.
We both sucked Polos to cancel the taste
But at least it was food and it filled the belly.

The set on the stage was a microwave oven.
The music was live and distractingly so,
Or had I forgotten *Macbeth* was by Brecht?
The art student witches were never a coven;
Macbeth wore braces and to what effect?
Half-baked like the pizza's cardboardy dough.

Hiyo Silver III

Lone Ranger says to Tonto,
"Do you speak Esperanto?
Because a desperado,
An evil-looking dago,
Is incommunicado
South of San Diego
With a million-dollar cargo
Stolen from Wells Fargo
En route from El Dorado,
'n' I gave my Spanish lexicon
To a hacienda-mender
Who hailed from Texicana,
An alcoholic Mexican
Who wore a red bandanna."

Says Tonto to Lone Ranger,
"You lead me into danger.
I speak your gringo lingo
And a patchy fake Apache
But no savvy Esperanto
So piss off, kemo sabay.
And who takes all the glory
For bourgeois law and order
At the end of each week's story?
Not Zorro's little sidekick,
Your obedient factotum.
So give me back my freedom,
My wigwam and my wampum.
I'm heading for the border . . ."

Sheriff and companion
Ride into the canyon.
In Tonto's tawny gullet
They find a silver bullet.

Another Country

Sketched by a thirsty watercolourist,
Kids on hind legs, miniature black goats,
Begged an olive for its greenest shoots.
Hens pecked at their own shadows in the dust.
And a girl came, as if from a taverna,
Holding a perfumed, sugar-powdered cake
And a glittering beaker of stone-cooled retsina.
The young man thanked her, drank and ate.
Her questions were incomprehensible,
So on his pad he wrote in Attic Greek
With a Made in England 2B Venus pencil:
γραφω ἀλλα οὐ φημι – I write but do not speak –
And her amazement at the oracle
Flattered his manhood like the alcohol.

Politics of Envy

In the Jackdaw folder of "Historical Genitalia",
The suitors of Elizabeth and reasons for their failure,
The Bonsai quality of Bonaparte's regalia,
What Hitler was missing in the region of Westphalia
Would all be investigated *inter* many *alia.*

Elizabeth I in a miniature by Hilliard
Scanned for masculinity by Hotson, Rowse and Tillyard,
The gusset of Napoleon expounded like the *Iliad,*
Hitler in his bunker playing pocket billiard
Would all be reproduced by the chiliad or milliard.

But if the young princess's *pudenda* were like Alice's
And only redetermined by Elizabethan malices,
If Bonaparte's was small because he owned huge palaces
And Hitler lost a ball when he gave the globe paralysis,
Do malicious jealousies provide all phallic fallacies?

The Fifth Column

The Fifth Column
between my legs,
the mauve toad
with hairy eggs,
garlic sausage
with an appetite,
my magic wand
of dynamite,
has this minute
commissioned me
to write his auto-
biography.

Blowing my Gaffe

You could have heard a pin drop
When I'd dropped that brick.
The pause was so pregnant
It started to be sick.

All eyes in the building
Were watching like a hawk's;
Some were out like organ stops,
The rest were out on stalks.

Mouths not gaping watered,
The breath they bated smelt.
Tongues would soon start wagging
Where butter wouldn't melt.

The smell of something brewing
Was worse than in a vat;
Some smelt something fishy,
Others smelt a rat.

Even those on tenterhooks
Were shaken to the core.
Those not shaken rigid
Made bee-lines for the door.

But did I bat an eyelid?
Did I turn a hair?
Though my heart was in my mouth
I beat it out of there.

Peace Talks

A tape-recorder would have bust a gut
To hear you say, "Why can't we just be friends?"
Scriptwriters would have groaned in unison.
But I had hopes, I tried to make amends;
I gave you tea and pleaded with you, but
Right from the start our peace talks were absurd.
For you said "Look" as soon as I said "Listen",
Then neither of us either watched or heard.

We were both diplomatic to a fault,
Postponing and evading the main issue
Till at last I asked you if you thought I loved you
And you said flatly, "Haven't got a clue."
That finished me. The conversation stalled.
You somehow managed to look satisfied
And took some Swiss Roll off the plate I shoved you,
While I felt half insulted I'd not cried.

Exile

The forest
Was what she missed most
From Czechoslovakia,
In the same way as we,
She supposed,
Would long for the sea.

But an island race
We already recall
Our maritime past
Of steam and sail
As if the sea air
Were as pure a memorial

As the land-locked
Hansel and Gretel
Pine forest smell.
Though inland in England
Woods swish in the wind
Like breakers on shingle,

And I, a Sassenach
With Gaelic names,
Surmise before me
An island's ancestry,
Forest and sea,
At the source of the Thames.

Eddystone Light

(for Debbie)

On the horizon
On a clear day,
The Eddystone
Rivets sea to sky;
A midnight sun
On summer nights,
It strokes a zone
With northern lights.

But a gale warning
Crackling with static
Talks the storm in
From mid-Atlantic,
And waves come ramming
The outcrop of rock
Where light's informing
On depth and dark.

A wave breaks high
On the lighthouse stone,
The sparks of spray
Spatter to foam,
And if land and sea
Share Genesis weather,
Why shouldn't we
Who chose each other?

Burrator Reservoir

We try to infer
The lie of the moorland
Before the river
And valley were drowned,
But we can see neither
The barrow nor tor
Burrator Reservoir
Was christened after.

Once in its reaches
When I was a boy
Black frogmen creatures
Bubbled all day
For a Dartmoor prisoner's
Stone-anchored corpse,
And for weeks foul waters
Tainted the taps.

And when in a war film
An airborne armada
Rained bomb after bomb
On Moehne and Eder,
I imagined the dam
At Burrator shatter
To a battering-ram
Of murderous water.

But now at this conduit
Constructed by man
From water and granite
With which Earth began,
We sense for a minute
Here at its crust
The death of a planet
Implicit in us.

Snow in the Night

Parting bright curtains
Transfigured by snowfall,
I stared through the windowpane's
Tearful cold oval

At mouldings, at sculpture
And chippings of air
Defining a blurred
Cleanliness everywhere.

Steaming like geysers
We went out when it stopped.
Miniature glaciers
Sparkled and dripped,

Shooting high scores
On the all-white target
Whose bull's-eyes they thawed
In the snow as we trudged it.

Powdery avalanches
Clumsily pounced
From twigs onto branches,
Fell prey to the ground.

Astonished we watched
The afternoon rescue
A Puritan-whitewashed
Devotional fresco

With evergreens brighter,
The sky more blue,
And us among nature
Invested as new.

The Touch

The Amphitheatre Entrance, Covent Garden.
Asked there for twopence for a cup of tea
The question smelt so methylated that
I both refused him change to buy his drink
And then the handshake which he offered me.
Though that was unforgivable, I think,
He shook his head and gave my arm a pat,
Able uncomprehendingly to pardon.

Later, on stage in a Verona square,
In came a dancer with a gammy leg,
In rags, on crutches, carrying a bowl
Among the corps de ballet idling there,
And though I knew that it was just a role,
I begged that he, though paid to, wouldn't beg.

London

Having classed it the dullest book I'd read
I now with eight million other extras work
On the set for the film of the London *A to Z.*
If only this part made my next a lead,
I'd like my office near St Paul's Cathedral
With its desk view of wind-gauges on cranes
Twiddled all working week by gusts that jerk
Company flags and liveried weather-vanes,
And free-range seagulls canting their dihedral
When gauged air currents tack or alter speed.
But I've checked the back of my swivel chair
And no sort of name but a brand name's there.

2, Church St.

Given our street-name, taxi-drivers grouse
That traffic there's re-routed almost daily.
Town-planners see located on our house
The foyer of their plush new library.
We and the landlord in the shop below
Are less progressive: for, though we both, I'm sure,
Will take the light-bulbs with us when we go,
We'd like a permanent crevasse next door.

Yet who could successfully keep as it is
This building of no public interest?
Give even the National Trust the premises
And where our doorbell-button was once pressed,
Turnstiles would click, and sight-seers would from there
Be shown the unused putty in my drawer,
The cooker kept in roped-off disrepair,
And your bike on a plinth outside the door.

But since it's valued solely for its bricks
Our house will soon be rubble in a basement.
Then all that is left will be the oral epics:
Our saga on the beer which refused to ferment,
The flood, the burglar, mildew, mice. Though later,
Not even aerial photography
Working with these folk memories as its data
Could prove that this was once our territory.

Breakwater, Plymouth

A mist as if the Channel were on fire
Dims the destroyer anchored in the Sound.
Nothing is as it seemed from the opposite shore:
The breakwater's as separate from its fort
As we two here at low tide on the sand.

We come out in the car to be alone
To beach, museum, harbour, zoo and tor
Like Dartmoor prisoners daily on the run,
And only find creations of despair,
Like the museum's most unsavoury one:

A guillotine carved lovingly in bone
By one of the French prisoners of war
Who mined and built the breakwater of stone.
But though a barrier can inhibit storms,
Can models of death be what his gifts were for?

Fire

It's company, she says,
As if the coal fire
Was a warm-hearted talker
From her part of Wales,
Or a genial smoker
Waiting for meals.

Each morning she stoops
And, setting aside
The blackened meshes,
Carries the still warm
Dust and ashes
Out of the widowed room.

Desert Island Disc

Ol' Man River. Sung by Paul Robeson and me.
He'd be the Mr Bass Man and Man Friday
To my Enrico Crusoe
And joining in the chorus . . . let me see . . .
High-day, freedom! Freedom, high-day!
Both the Douanier and Jean-Jacques Rousseau.

Smell the sea-island cotton and the sea.
But look – who's there in that dug-out canoe?
The hungry, aging hippy
Looks like my father but it might be me
Seeking self-knowledge in an old *Who's Who*
And droning on about the Mississippi.

Watershed

The Bow River. Bow River.
Three men in his anecdote,
One with an artificial leg,
Were heading for rapids in a boat
On the Bow River. Or wherever.
Vague memories of lake and muskeg
In the Arctic Watershed
Looked for a Bow to rediscover.
Is that in Canada? I said.

Rocky Mountains. Banff, Alberta.
I know it, yes, and Lake Louise.
A girl, the current and a canoe
Are moving with me past dark trees
Once more into the unlived future
Fifteen or sixteen summers ago
One summer evening, almost night,
On cold coppery-green melt-water
Which I thought I would never forget.

Driftwood

Her third child, a baby daughter,
The love-child of her thirties, gone.
The carrycot gone from its transporter.
Before she could dial 999
The bell grew angry with the phone
And a male voice came on the line
Inviting her to a tall thin house
In one of the older terraces
To a party where her bravest face
Searched the cigarette smoke and glasses
For the villain of the piece,
Until a suit-and-tie man said
That yes he knew where her daughter was
If they could reach her before high tide.

Wearing her black shoes on her hands,
In a seascape grey and middle-aged,
She walked for miles on narrowing sands,
But no sign. Nothing. The stranger followed.
Suddenly, pointing up the beach,
She ran on, shouted back, then waded
Out to a carrycot cauled in seaweed
And inside – oh, if only . . . maybe . . .
Floating jerkily in the shallows
The dead shape of a sleeping baby
Whose warm body, blushing head
Felt like suede and smelt of shortbread,
Opened its hungry mouth and cried,
Before them both, before high tide.

European Games

Remembering the agony and triumph,
The three perform the medal ceremony
As if it were a sporting version of
The Crucifixion or Transfiguration,
And like a Christmas tree with chocolate money,
The solemn victor wears his decoration,
The gold he plundered from the enemy.
Three flags ascend to his national anthem,
A brassy dance tune. In the setting sun
The shadows of the flags all look the same.

Longlevens Poems

1 *Introducing Little Normans*

Montfort, Mortimer, Mainard, Beaumont,
What do the streetnames have in common?
I've cracked the code. They're Norman surnames.
The estate was christened Little Normans
After the farm it housed and gardened.
The suburb sprawl is named Longlevens.

No need to visit us to know the place.
Do rotary driers, flowering cherries,
Integral garages, car shampoos,
And houses that the builders must have cloned
Stand for a culture that you cannot stand?
Well, that's Flatfallows, Black&Deckerland.

2 Pongs

The Black&Deckerlander proudly smells
Expensive pungencies of smokeless fuels,
The tasty flavours of the neighbour's meals.

But behind frosted glass the aerosols
Chosen to match hand-towels and toilet rolls
Betray the offensive movements of the bowels.

The turds not misbehaving in the bowl
(The worry bead, the sausage stuck to grill –
You know the types) are not flushed far afield.

From our back gardens, we can see the Muck Farm
And if the wind's NE, the weather warm,
It is as if we faced the city's bum

After it's fed on eggs, chips, beans and peas.
Lilies of the valley cannot sweeten marsh gas.
The double glazing has its other uses.

3 Longlevens Sunsets

The sunsets here can be spectacular.
The sun glows like the planet Jupiter,
The sky a blue and crimson watercolour,
Clouds, Arctic islands above Canada.
The westward-facing windows of the houses
Are stained glass and the walls are murals.
Or is it that the sun each evening blushes
At the bare pink brickwork of our mortgaged morals?

4 Sex in the Suburbs

Leaning on bikes against a bungalow
Two boys were peeping through the bathroom window.
I glared at them till they were forced to go.

The lady of the house, if she it was,
Is short and dumpy and she wears long dresses.
She buys Martini at the local grocer's.

I think of her and I am the voyeur:
She soaps her buttocks as I watch the water
Drip from her dark isosceles of fur.

5 Sanctuary

Seagulls in a loose V-formation
Fly in squadrons over the estate
Westwards on winter evenings to the Severn.
The Estuary, no doubt. Mudflats at sunset.
Buffeted by winds the seagulls rally.
Caught by the rain they hold their courses firm.
Tinted by sunlight they move comfortably,
And every evening I look up to them
As fly-pasts for the men returning home.

6 *Dirty Work*

On Wednesdays, if we're lucky,
Bohemian down-and-outs,
Piratical suntanned men
Tattooed and wearing hats
Come to empty the bins.

They leave the area mucky,
And grumbling to ourselves
We men clear up the rubbish
Like houseproud downtrodden wives
Snubbed for being snobbish.

7 *The Field*

A pasture without cows, an urban field,
A paddock grazing no gymkhana ponies.
A hedge on one side, gardens on the other,
A no man's land between the town and country.
Teenagers escape here during *Crossroads*
For calf-love, horseplay or a quiet smoke.
They lounge around in boots and faded denim
Like cow-hands in a sunset on a Western.
Their bikes lie in the grass, the handlebars
Horns on a herd of new metallic cattle.

8 Little Normans Stereo System

Listen to Little Normans on cassette:
The fuzzy glockenspiel of an ice cream van
Playing "Greensleeves" *con moto* in short bursts.
Homeric heroes on their motorbikes.
The squeal of guinea pigs eager to be fed
On squeaking outer leaves of cabbages.
The starlings twittering and the children's clamour.
Occasional light aircraft overhead.

And do you long for noises you can choose?
The conversations of celebrities,
Laughter, bullets, music, sport, applause,
Police-car sirens in Los Angeles,
Accents that suffer, warn, insult, accuse?
Then join the club until the Late Night News.

A White Christmas

And is it a year ago now
that you and I as we were
played our *Dr Zhivago,*

Lara and Omar Sharif
walking in snow on snow
and wondering what to believe?

Birds of brilliant plumage
roosted upside down
over butchers' carnage.

Conspirators in a café
at the Swiss centre of town,
we warmed our hands on the coffee.

The waitress with her notepad
scribbled our printable copy.
The rest was off the record:

thoughts for the Thought Police,
enormities accomplished
but for the time and place.

Later, in a churchyard,
we wandered like two penguins
on a charity Christmas card;

the backview of divinities
in the stained-glass windows
glinted like black ice,

and with us in the porch
wind and snow sought sanctuary
in the locked door of the church.

We stood there talking steam
like guests late for a wedding
married in an Arctic dream

with snowflakes for confetti,
but no photographer
no priest no wedding party

and so when we kissed goodbye
we made separate tracks across
the drifts of the cemetery,

longing a year ago
for the candleflames of the crocus
after deadening snow.